MONT

A POSTCARD BOOK

PHOTOGRAPHY BY MICHAEL S. SAMPLE

FALCON™

Helena, Montana

Copyright © by Falcon Press® Publishing Co., Inc., Helena and Billings, Montana.

Design, typesetting, and other composition work by Falcon Press Publishing Co., Inc., Helena, Montana. Printed in Korea.

ISBN: 1-56044-195-X

Falcon Press publishes a wide variety of Montana books and calendars. For a free catalog, write Falcon Press, P.O. Box 1718, Helena, Montana 59601, or call toll-free 1-800-582-2665.

Front Cover: Reynolds Creek in Glacier National Park

These slightly oversized postcards require first-class postage.

MONTANA

The bitterroot is Montana's state flower. It was first collected in 1806 by Captain Meriwether Lewis of the Lewis and Clark Expedition, in what is now the Bitterroot Valley.

Photo by Michael S. Sample

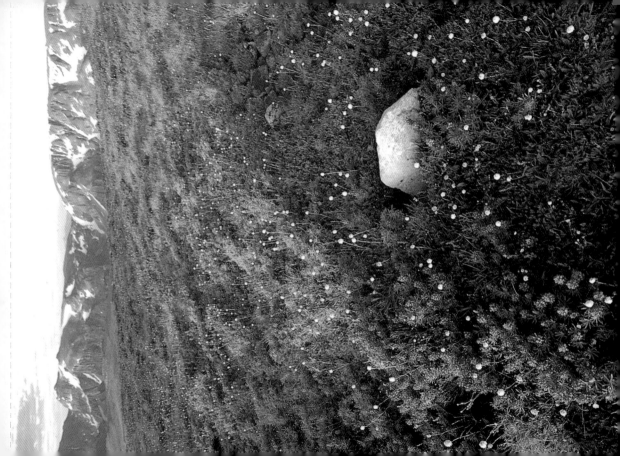

MONTANA

Alpine flowers blanket the Hellroaring Plateau in Montana's
Absaroka-Beartooth Wilderness. The 920,400-acre
wilderness forms the northern border of
Yellowstone National Park.

Photo by Michael S. Sample

MONTANA

A large rainbow trout feeds at Giant Springs Heritage State
Park near Great Falls, Montana. The park features the
largest freshwater spring in the United States.

Photo by Michael S. Sample

MONTANA

Winter settles on the ranch country of the Big Hole Valley,
a rich grassland surrounded by rugged mountains in
southwestern Montana.

MONTANA

Picturesque badlands interrupt the prairie in eastern
Montana. Carved by water and wind, badlands and
"breaks" form colorful, rugged landscapes in this
land of far horizons.

Photo by Michael S. Sample

MONTANA

Snow-capped peaks crown the autumn splendor of
St. Mary Lake in Glacier National Park, Montana. The
park's soaring mountains inspired early visitors to call it
the "Crown of the Continent."

Photo by Michael S. Sample

MONTANA

The steep sides and jagged summit of 10,157-foot Trapper
Peak are framed by a ponderosa pine in Montana's
Bitterroot National Forest.

Photo by Michael S. Sample

MONTANA

A cow elk nuzzles her calf in a meadow of shimmering
foxtail barley. Elk are found throughout the mountains of
western Montana and in a few locations in the
eastern part of the state.

Photo by Michael S. Sample

MONTANA

The pristine waters of the North Fork of the Blackfoot River
flow through the Scapegoat Wilderness in Lolo National
Forest, northeast of Helena, Montana.

Photo by Michael S. Sample

MONTANA

The Crazy Mountains, one of the largest areas of exposed volcanic rock in Montana, rise above cattle country north of Big Timber.

Photo by Michael S. Sample

MONTANA

The sun sets on Stoney Indian Peaks in Glacier National
Park, Montana. The Stonies were Assiniboine Indians
whose name came from their practice of
cooking on heated stones.

Photo by Michael S. Sample

MONTANA

Palisade Falls plummets eighty feet in Gallatin National
Forest's Hyalite Canyon. The canyon is a popular
recreational area south of Bozeman, Montana.

MONTANA

Horses in southeastern Montana enjoy the warmth of
a summer day on prairie hills near the Little Bighorn
Battlefield National Monument.

Photo by Michael S. Sample

MONTANA

A morning mist rises and reveals the colors of autumn in a
forest in northwestern Montana. Fifteen species of conifers
alone can be found in this area.

Photo by Michael S. Sample

MONTANA

The Mission Mountains rise above a flower-filled meadow
in Montana's Swan Valley. The Missions are a popular
hiking and backpacking area between the Swan and
Flathead valleys.

Photo by Michael S. Sample

MONTANA

Granite Peak, the highest peak in Montana at 12,799 feet,
cradles one of several glaciers in the Absaroka-Beartooth
Wilderness. The wilderness contains 28 peaks over
12,000 feet in elevation.

Photo by Michael S. Sample

MONTANA

Showy heartleaf arnica and Indian paintbrush add
color to a late summer snowfall at Logan Pass in
Glacier National Park, Montana.

Photo by Michael S. Sample

MONTANA

Bison cows and a calf are home on the National Bison
Range near Moiese, Montana. A herd of approximately
500 bison share the 18,500-acre preserve with elk,
bighorn sheep, and antelope.

Photo by Michael S. Sample

MONTANA

Soaring to 10,969 feet, Emigrant Peak looms above
a channel of the Yellowstone River in Paradise Valley,
south of Livingston, Montana.

Photo by Michael S. Sample

MONTANA

Pebble Creek winds beneath Cutoff Mountain on a winter
day in the northern part of Yellowstone National Park.
This area is crossed by a year-round road that goes from
Gardiner, Montana, to Cooke City, Montana.

Photo by Michael S. Sample

MONTANA

Reynolds Creek cascades over angular rocks near Logan
Pass in Glacier National Park, Montana. Logan Pass is the
summit of the park's famous Going-to-the-Sun Road.

Photo by Michael S. Sample

MONTANA

A curious grizzly cub in northwestern Montana rises on its
hind legs to get a better look. Montana supports the largest
grizzly bear population in the lower 48 states.

Photo by Michael S. Sample

DISCOVER MONTANA

There's no time like the present to get out and sample
Montana's recreational opportunities.

LET FALCON BE YOUR GUIDE

For a free catalog of books, maps and other Montana products, please send in this card
with the following information:

Name _____

Address _____

City _____ State _____ Zip _____

Or call 1-800-582-2665

FALCON™

BUSINESS REPLY MAIL

FIRST-CLASS MAIL PERMIT NO 80 HELENA MT

POSTAGE WILL BE PAID BY ADDRESSEE

FALCON DIRECT
PO BOX 1718
HELENA MT 59624-9948